Life in the Mountains

Bull Moose

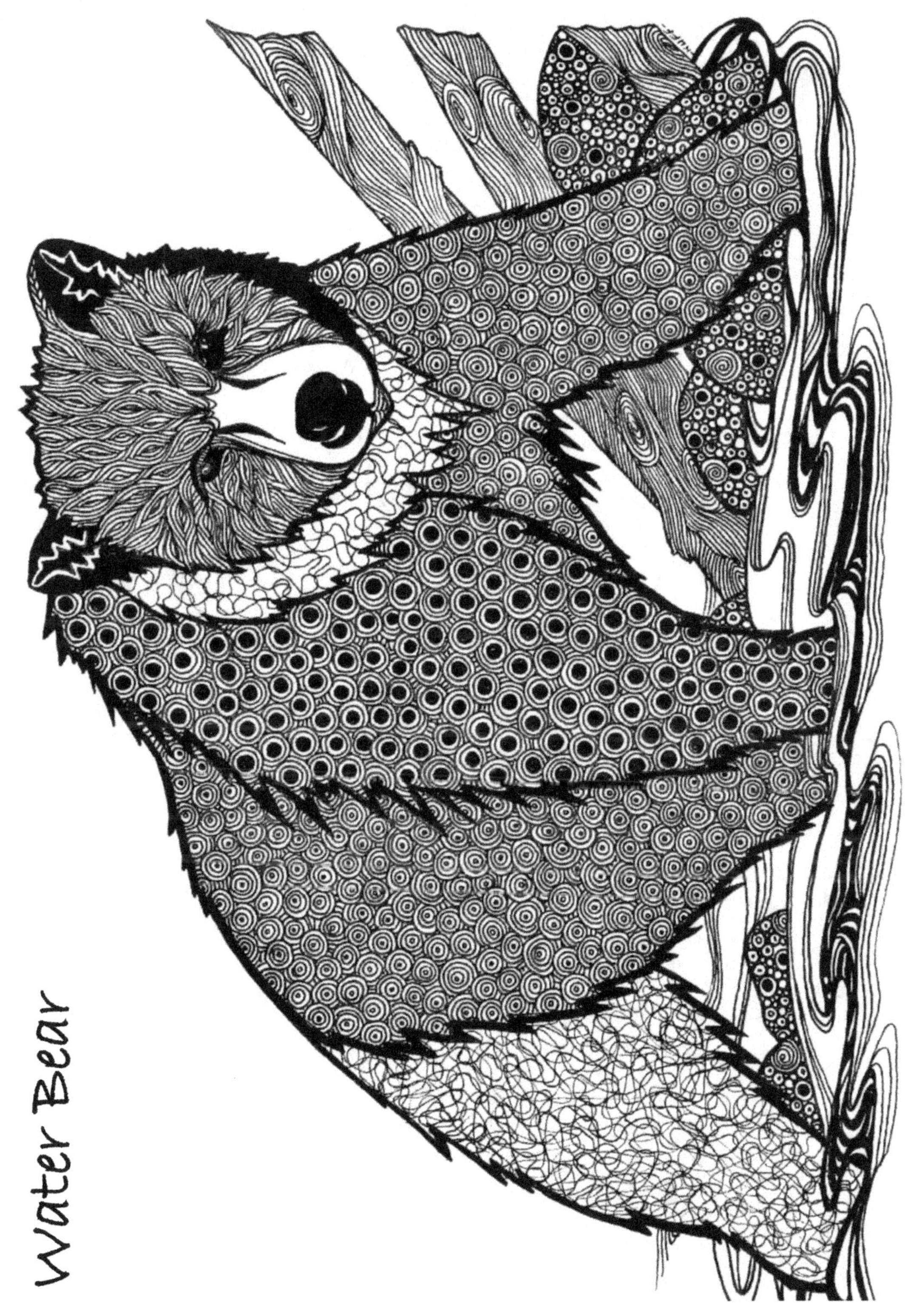

Water Bear

Stellar Blue Jay

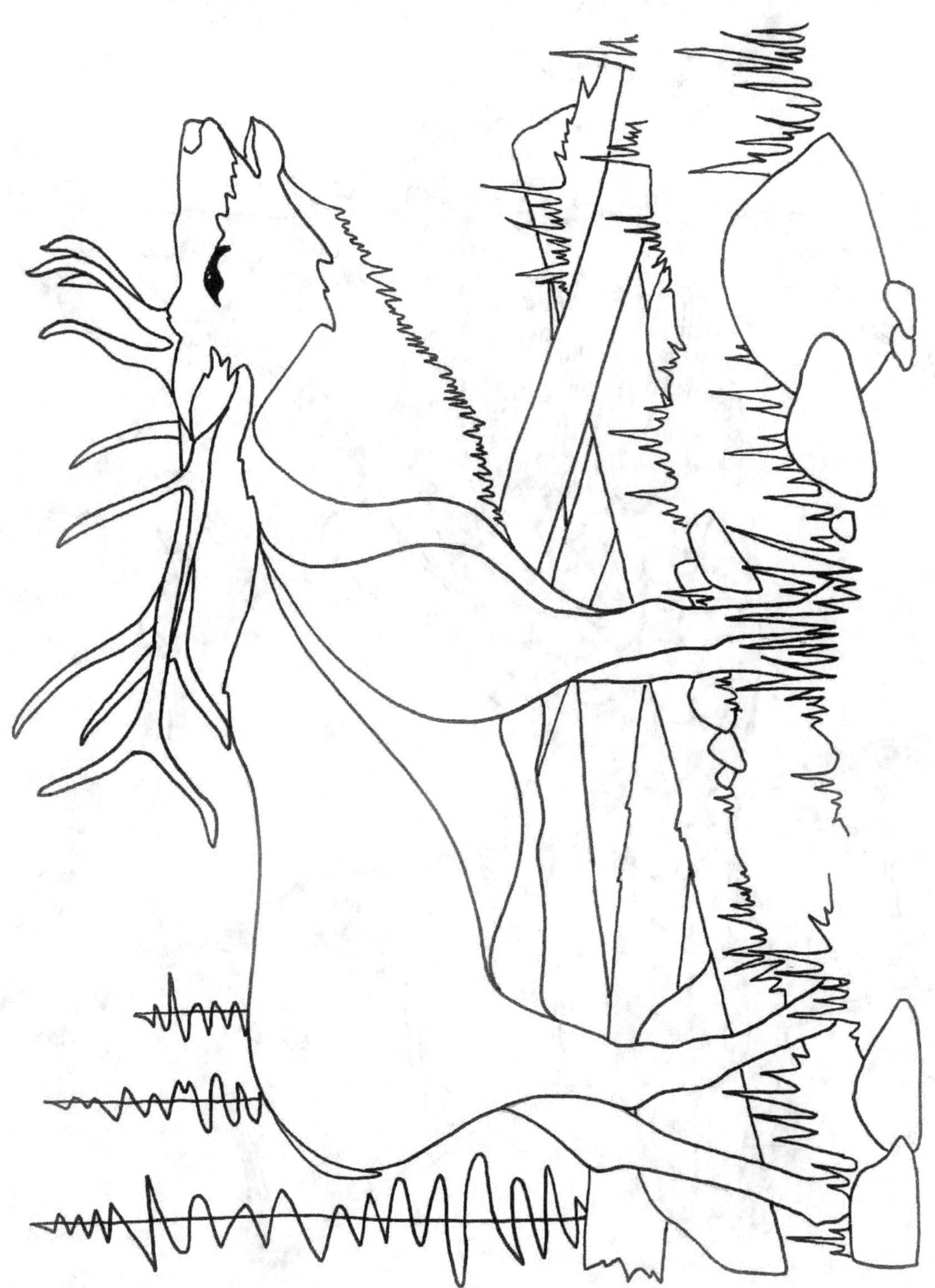

Bull Elk

Beaver

Wolf in Aspens

Berry Bear

Raven

Lynx in Sticks

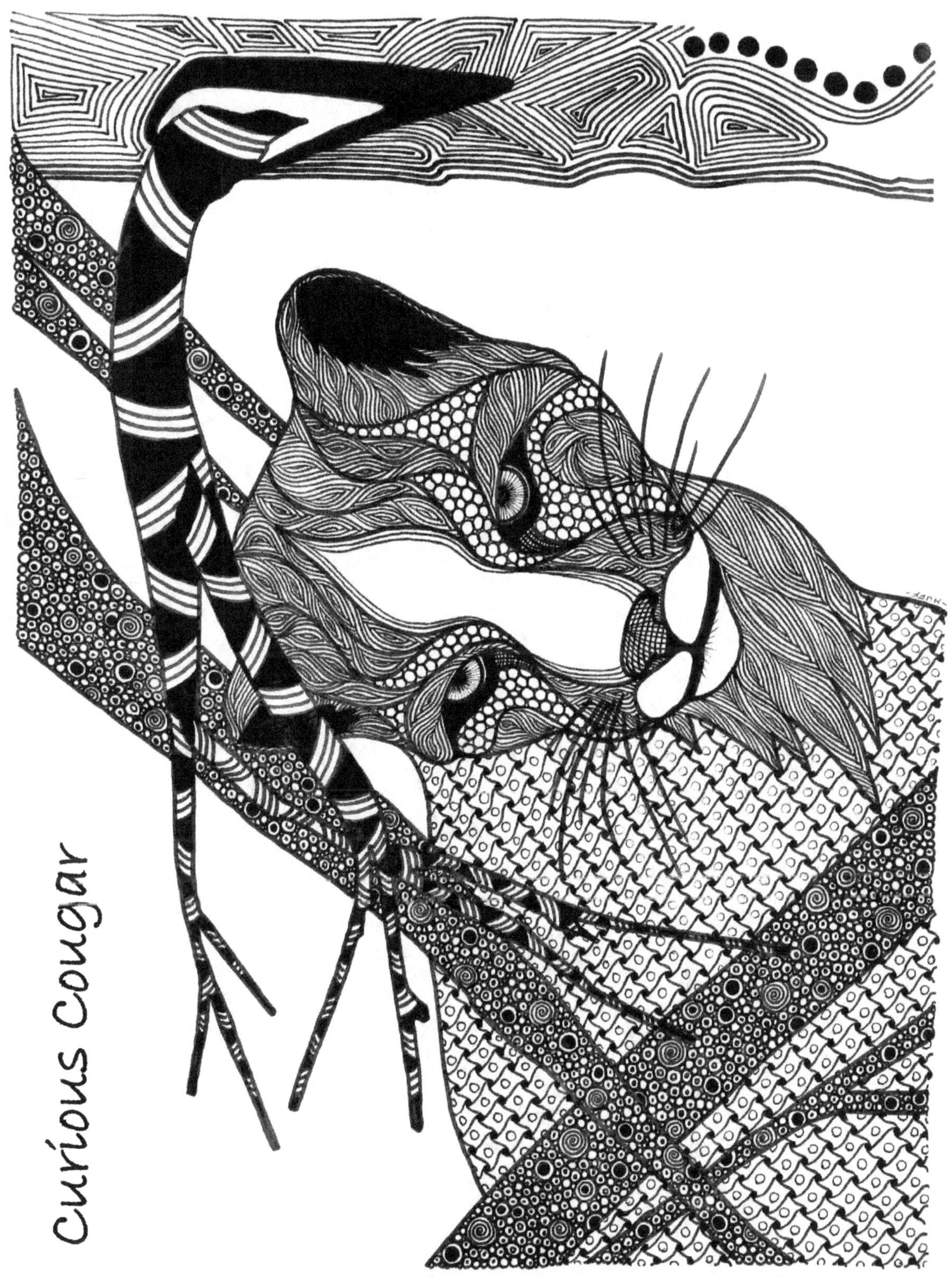

Curious Cougar

Owl

Squirrel

Buck Deer

Squirrel on a limb

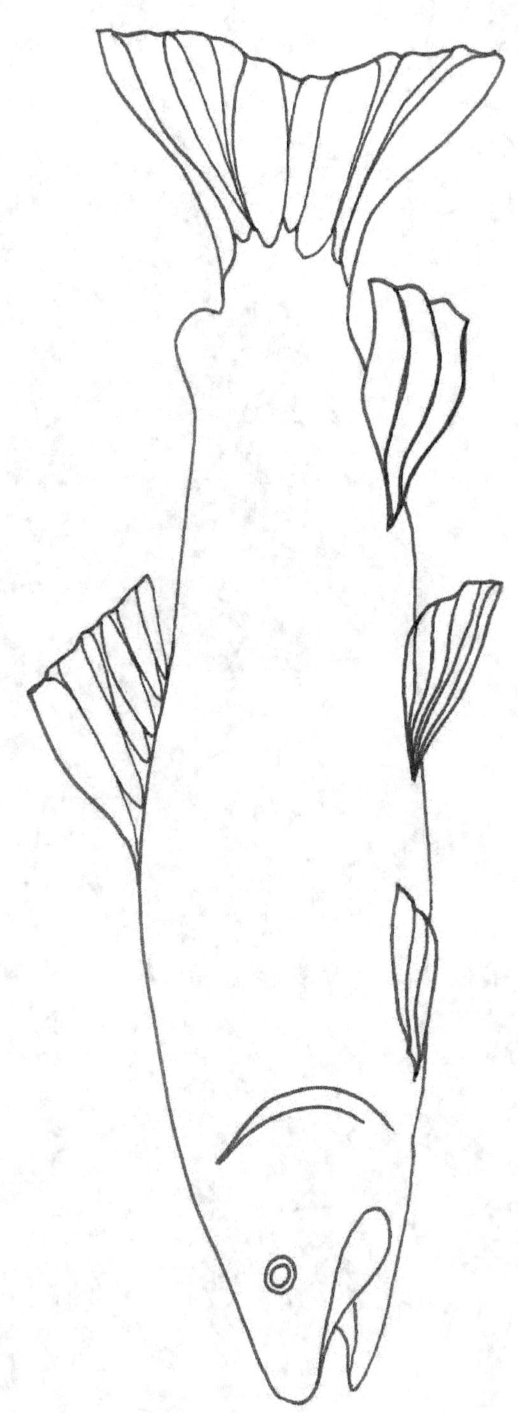

Dream Fish

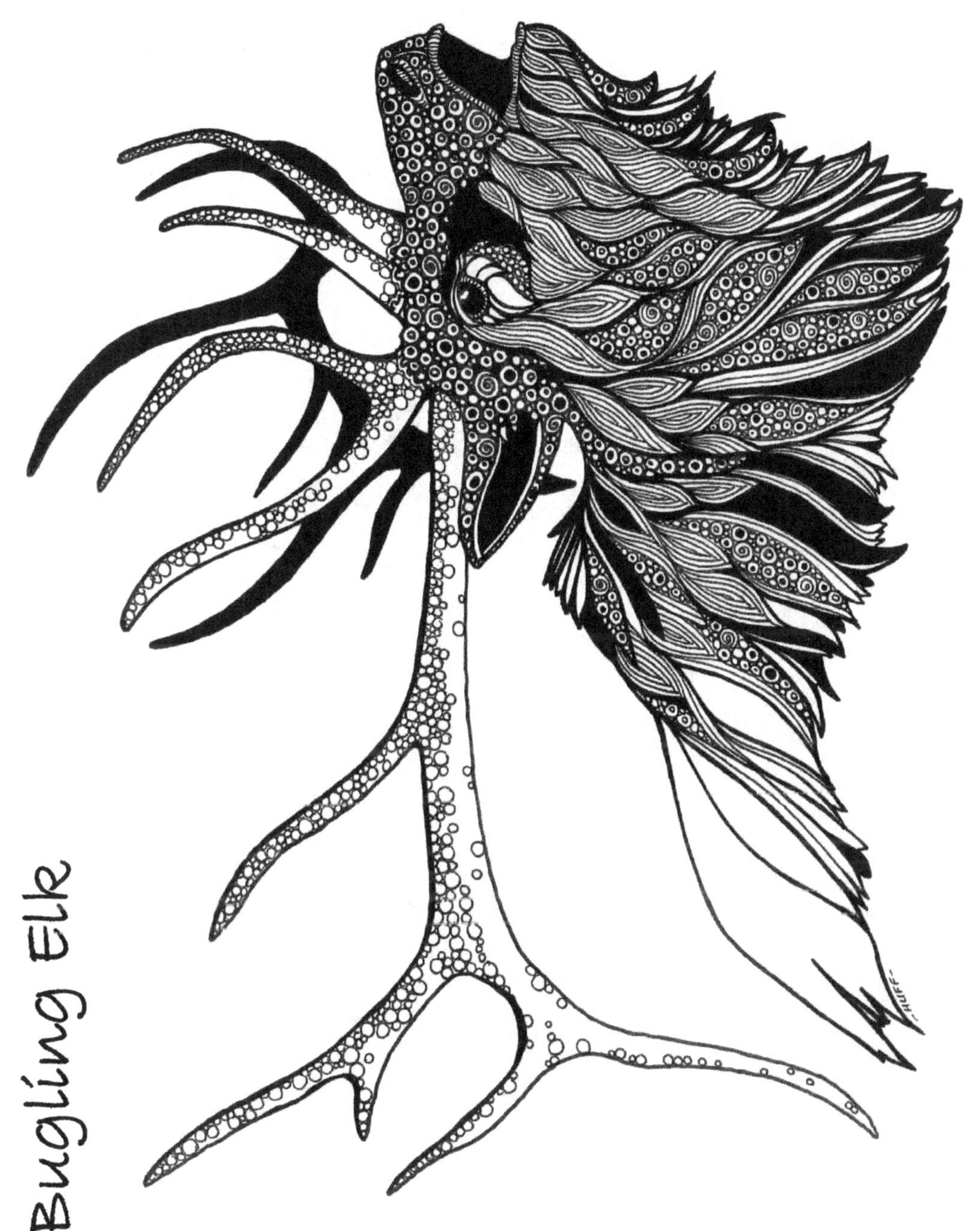

Bugling Elk

Big Horn Sheep

Long Ear Rabbit

Splashing Moose

Bald Eagle

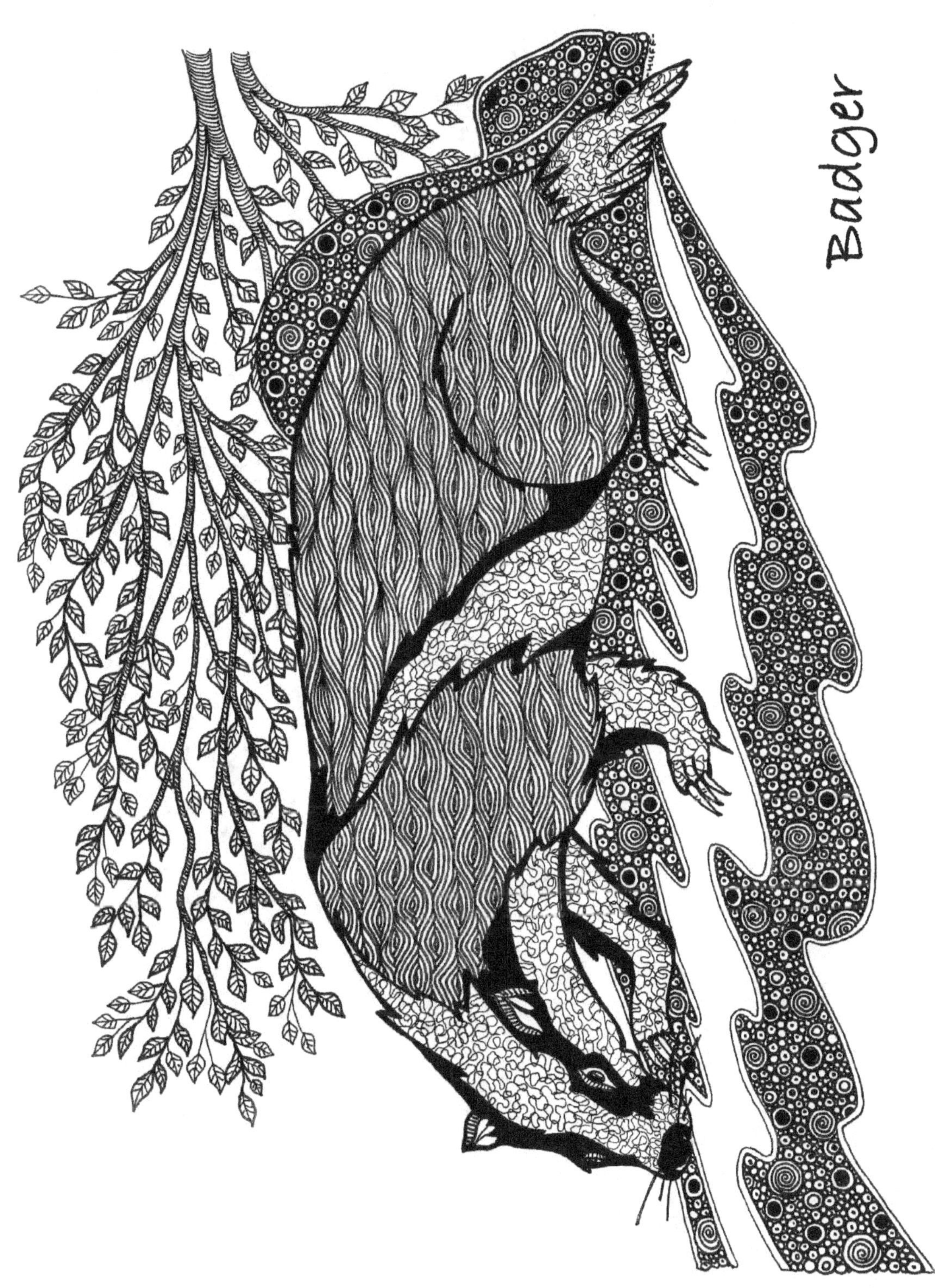

Badger

Bison on the Range

Mule Deer in Winter

Fawn Love

Pronghorn Antelope

Peaceful Swan

Sleeping Fox

Deer Mouse

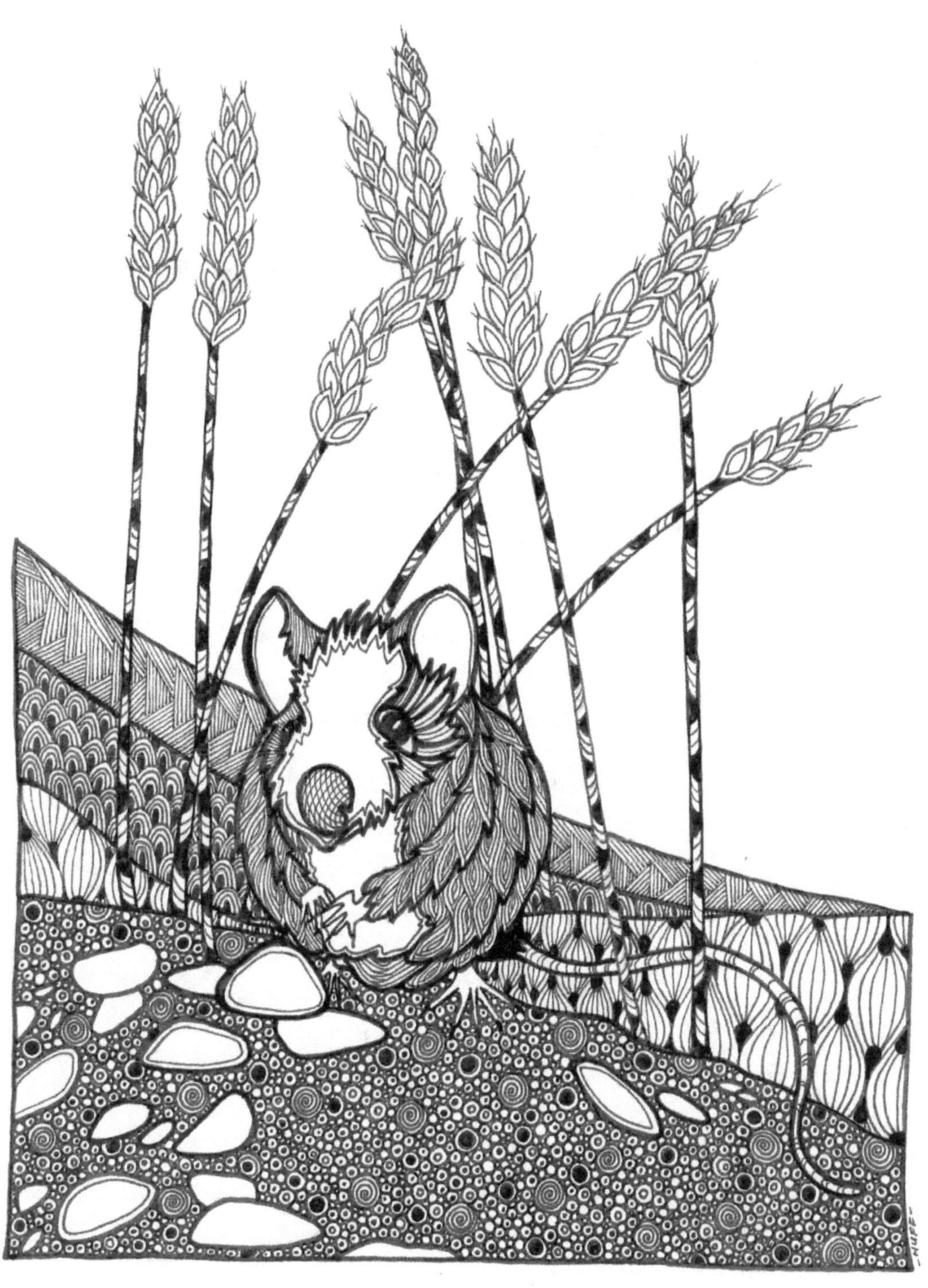

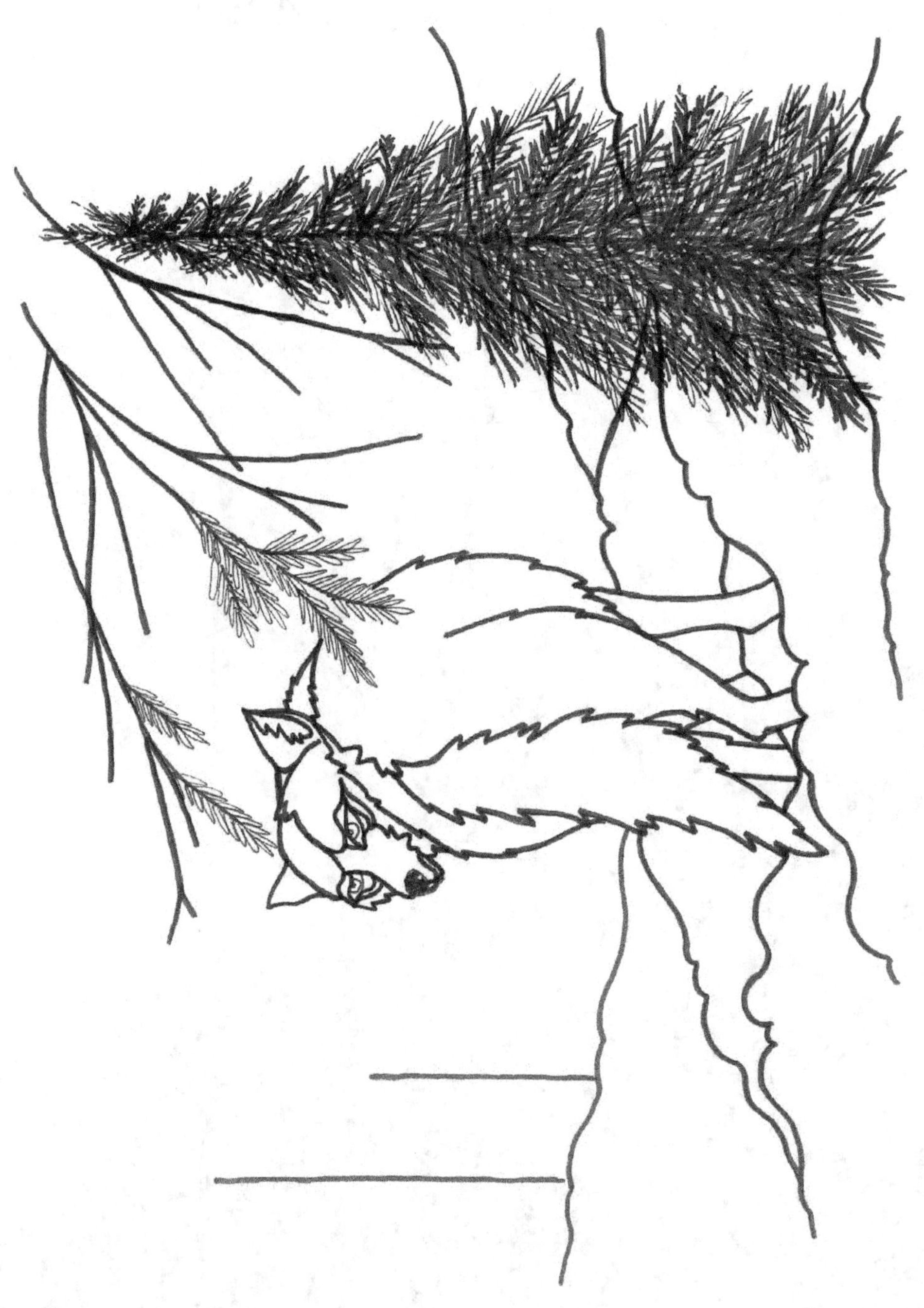

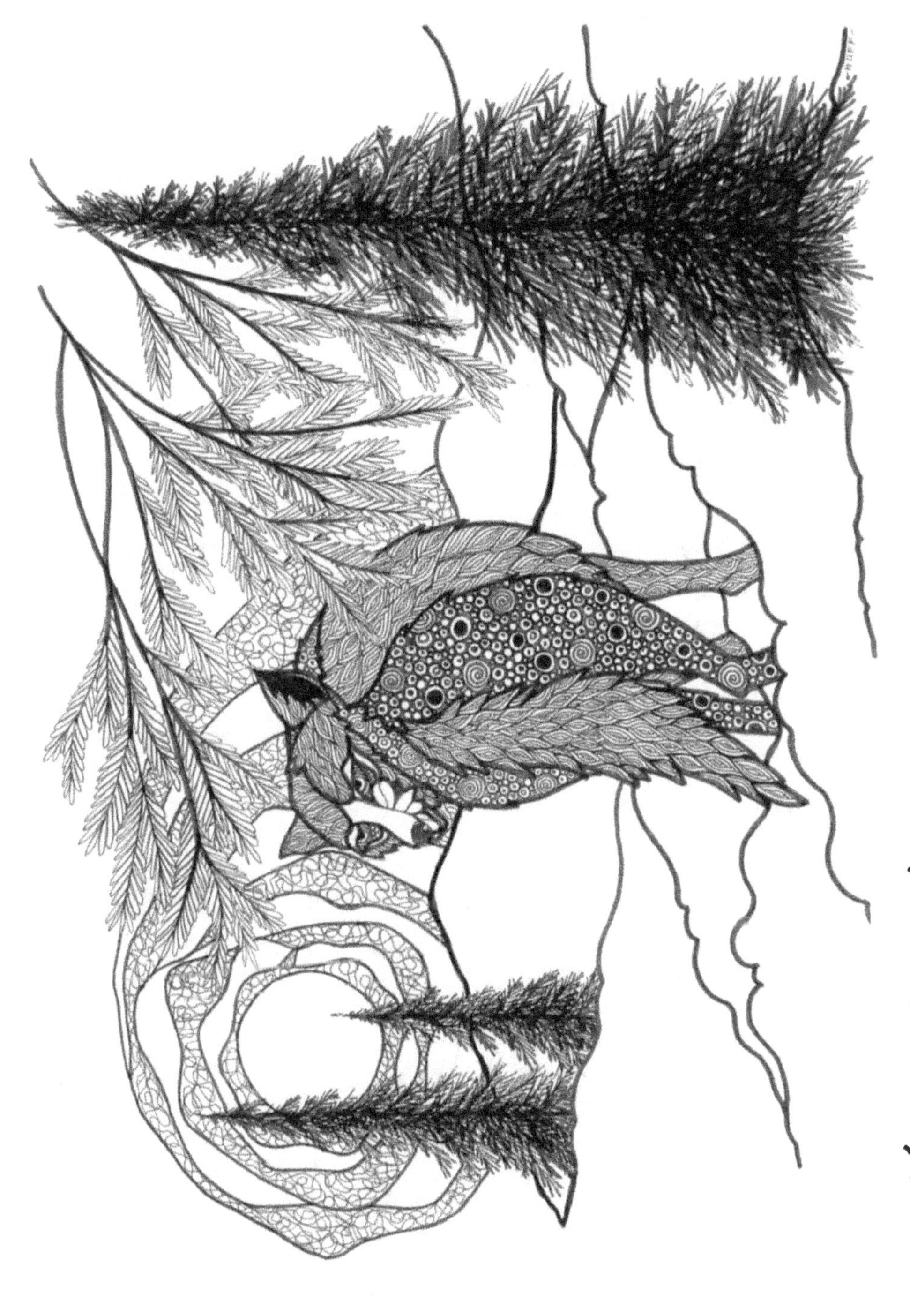

Cautious Coyote

Standing Moose

Thinking Bear

Majestic Big Horn Sheep

Raccoon

Baby Red Foxes

Buffalo Wild

Skunk in Roses

Grouse in Berries

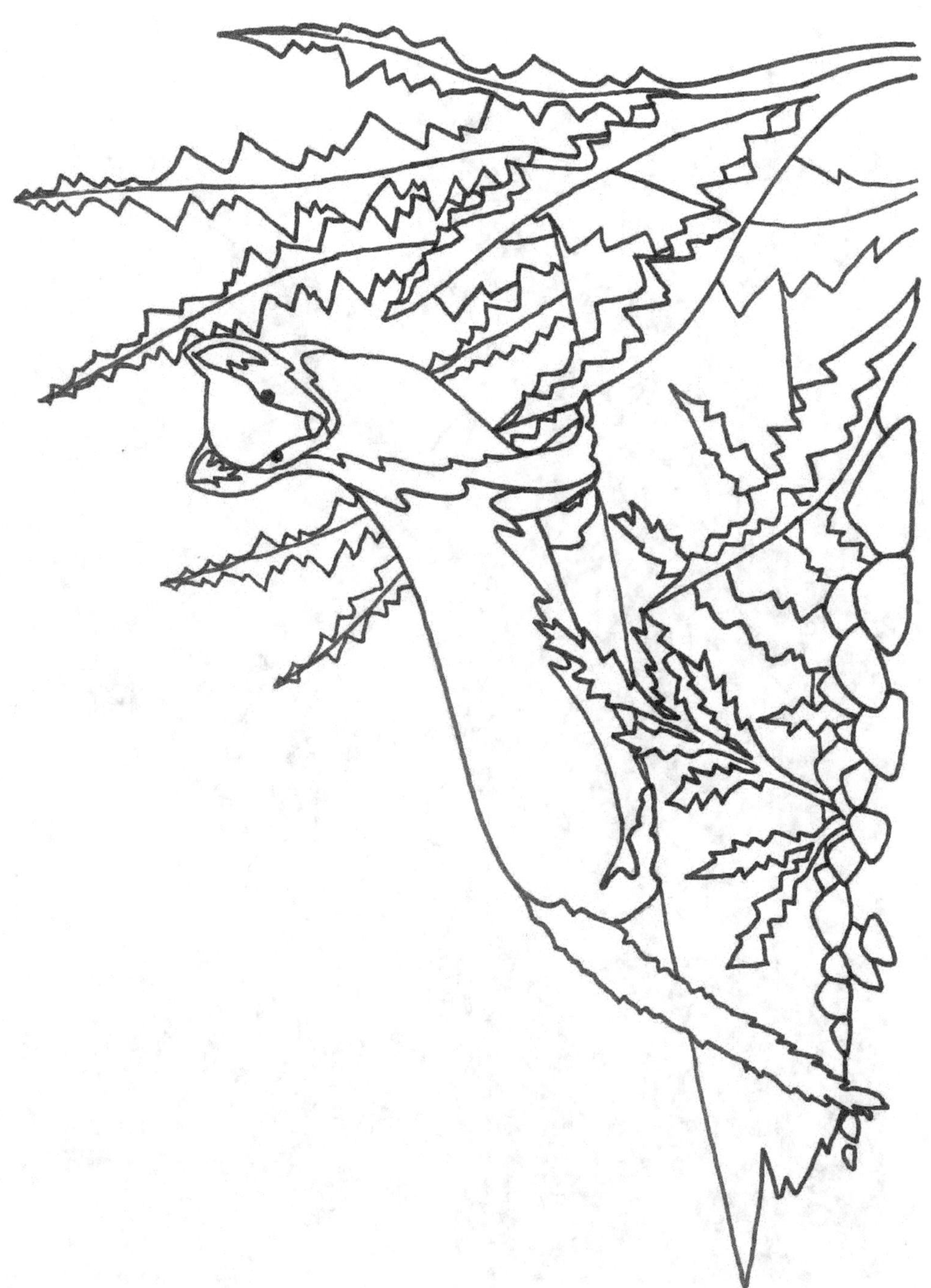

Weasel

Golden Mantle Squirrel

Sitting Bear

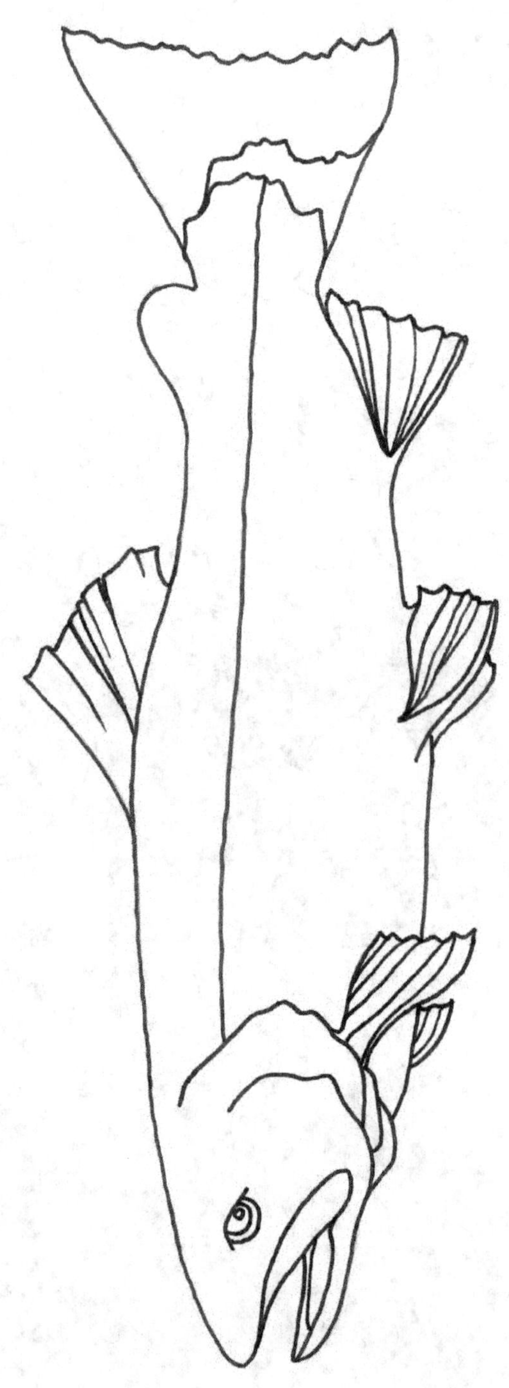

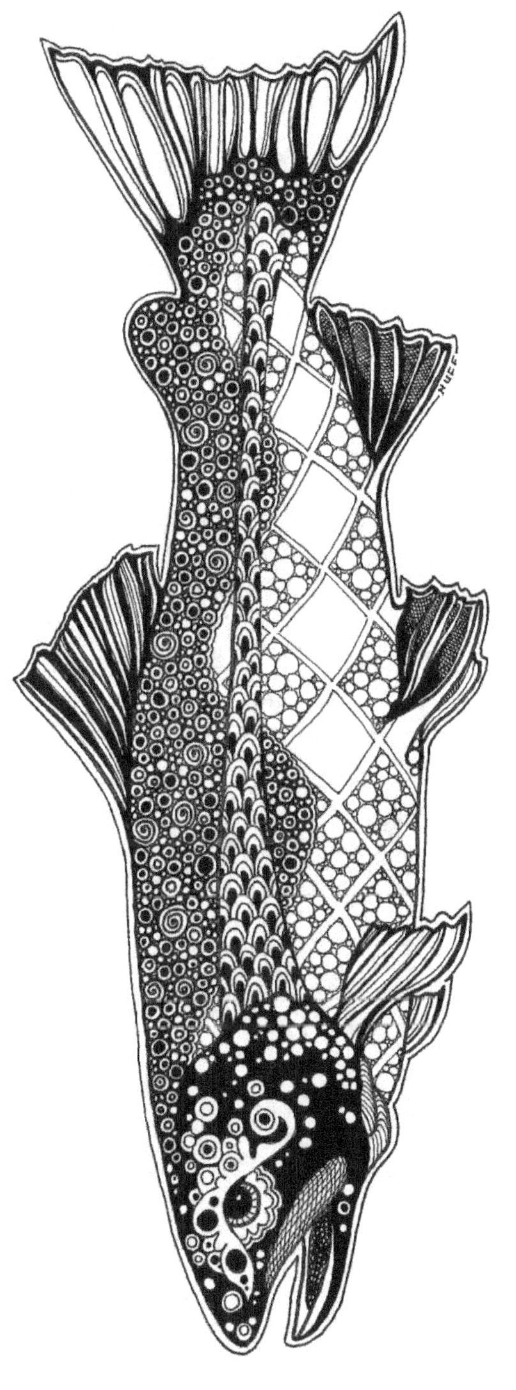

Over the Rainbow Trout

Dragonfly and Iris

RACCOON

Butterfly

Jumping Jack Rabbit

Grazing Mountain Goat

Smiling Fox

Chickadees